What Is a Mammal?

Janet Carson

Rosen Classroom Books and Materials
New York

Some mammals are small.

A mouse is a mammal.

Some mammals are big. An
elephant is a mammal.

Some mammals live on the land.
A giraffe is a mammal.

Some mammals live in the water.

A whale is a mammal.

Most mammals have fur on their bodies. A cow is a mammal.

A mammal keeps the same body heat most of the time. A bear is a mammal.

Mammals feed their babies milk from their bodies. Monkeys are mammals.

Most mammals give **birth** to live babies. Horses are mammals.

All mammals **breathe** air. A dog is a mammal.

People are mammals, too!

Glossary

birth   The act of coming into life.

breathe   To take air into your body and send it back out.